Dragons Of The World And Where They Roam

Carsten R Jorgensen

Written and published in Canada.

ISBN: 0-9949338-5-1
ISBN-13: 978-0-9949338-5-0

CONTENTS

ACKNOWLEDGMENTS

My appreciation goes to Dana Woodard for editing this work and for editing the pictures. Thank you Dana for your work on this manuscript.

(All images in this book are known or thought to be public domain except where stated otherwise and permission was granted.)

Cover Design by Dana Woodard
Wood Carved Dragon on cover created by Terry O'Sullivan

1 INTRODUCTION

Today everybody has heard of dragons. They are huge fire breathing creatures that can fly on mighty wings. They are found in fairy tales and in modern stories. In Peter Jackson's movie 'The Hobbit' the dragon Smaug accumulated riches in gold and silver and attacked Lake Town with its fiery breath. Dragons are also shown in other movies such as 'Eragon', 'How To Train Your Dragon', 'The Never Ending Story', 'Dragonslayer', 'The Flight Of Dragons', 'Dragonheart', and the TV series 'Game of Thrones'. Dragons are accepted today as creatures of myth and legend.

Despite the common theory that dragons are only mythical, there are reports of dragons in our present times. Reports of dragons date back centuries and have been noted in accounts of Aristotle, the Bible, the vikings, as well as many other civilizations and throughout many eras.

Many types of dragons, in particular the water dragons, remain in the world today. They are elusive and most people are not likely to see them, but they do exist.

2 THE CLASSIFICATION OF DRAGONS

Athanasius Kircher (1601 to 1680) was a biologist who studied dragons in nature. He also did some classifications and examined fossil bones. From his studies he wrote the book, "A Natural History Of Dragons". Athanasius wrote his book in Latin, however, the book is now owned by Darius Matthias Klein who translated it and had it copyrighted.

There are many different types and species of dragons. Thus they also vary in size. Some are quite small and some are huge. The young dragons are hatched from eggs.

Kircher's illustrations of dragons and other animals.

Fire dragons are omnivores eating both meat and vegetable matter and fruit. These dragons have two types of teeth. Sharp teeth for tearing meat and flat teeth to eat vegetable matter and fruits.

Birds have two types of stomachs, the regular stomach and the gizzard. The birds swallow small stones which go to the gizzard where they are used for grinding down hard food items like seeds and nuts. Similar to birds, the dragons grind down rocks with their flat teeth and these ground down rocks also assist the dragon to grind down tough parts of their food, like bones, which they have swallowed with the meat.

Parts of these ground up rock would become stuck in their teeth. The dragon will have left over food in its stomach after digestion. Bacteria decomposes these food remains and produce hydrogen and methane gasses. In humans these gasses are released by burping to prevent the intestinal tract from becoming bloated and causing stomach cramps. In the dragon these gasses are ejected into a storage sack. When the gasses are ejected from the storage sack they are ignited by the rock and mineral particles stuck in the dragon's teeth. Thus the exhale from the storage sack results in an emission of fire.

Another example we find of a creature using a hot, noxious spray for defense in nature is the Bombardier Beetle. There are hundreds of types of Bombardier Beetles all over the world with various defense mechanisms.

"Bombardier beetle" from India

This beetle uses a mixture of two enzymes, hydroquinone and hydrogen peroxide that it mixes together inside two chambers, causing the mixture to heat to nearly 100 °C. The larger, inner chamber empties into the smaller outer one. Heat from the reaction brings the mixture to near the boiling point of water and produces gas that drives the ejection through an opening near the anus.

Some Bombardier Beetles can direct the spray over a wide range of directions. With a popping sound and a puff of what looks like smoke, the Bombardier Beetle can fire more than 20 times at its enemies. The damage caused can be fatal to some attacking insects.

A second classification of dragons is the water dragon. These are the sea serpents. In Norway, Sweden and Denmark water dragons were called Lindorm or Lindworm. The term "Orm" is translated as "worm" in English but it is also the word for "a dragon". They were called Orm because they have the same shape as earth worms, only of course they are much bigger.

There were Lindorms which were not aquatic. Some of the terrestrial Lindorms were just called Orms.

Orms were of different species. Some types of Orm had four legs and no wings, some had two legs near the head and no wings, and some species had wings.

The Orm was a cave dweller. If it could find no cave to inhabit, it would dig out a cave for itself in the side of a hill. The worm shape of its body made it ideal to burrow underground.

As well as fire dragons, there were dragons that did not breathe fire. There were some dragons that spat poison; very much like the cobra snake which spits lethal venom.

Some dragons living in caves had hoards of gold and silver. These dragons were attracted to bright shiny objects, picked them up, and took them to their lairs in their cave homes. Magpies and ravens do so as well. A raven will pick up a shiny object such as a spoon or a piece of jewelry and fly to its nest where it will keep it. There are many stories of people who have found very valuable items in a raven's nest. In the movie 'The Hobbit' the dragon Smaug had a very great hoard inside the Lonely Mountain.

3 TALES OF DRAGONS

Before historical times, the countries were smaller than today. Families counted their ancestry through the females not the males. In royalty, it was usually the firstborn princess who inherited the kingdom. The sons of kings would leave the kingdom when they reached manhood. A prince would go out to find his fortune.

The hopes of the young prince was to find a kingdom which needed a king. There, he would marry the crown princess and eventually become king. These stories are now found in collections of what are called fairy tales. Two examples are 'Sleeping Beauty' and 'Snow White'. In these two stories the prince had an easy time. All the prince had to do was to kiss the princess. In most kingdoms the young prince would have to fight and kill a dragon to gain the hand of the princess.

In some countries, the dragon would eat people unexpectedly. To prevent these unexpected attacks, the king would decree that at regular intervals a person was to be chained to a rock or a post as an offering to the dragon. In many stories the sacrificed person was to be a young maiden. Eventually the citizens would revolt and demand that the next offering was to be the king's own daughter. Therefore, in many stories, the traveling prince would find the princess chained to the post or rock. There, the prince killed the dragon and set the princess free. The princess then married the prince and the prince would become the next king when the old king died.

"Ruggiero Rescuing Angelica" an illustration of
Ludovico Ariosto's "Orlando Furioso".

Artwork by Gustav Doré (1832–1883)

4 ALF AND ALFHILD

Since there were dragons of various sizes, some people would keep a dragon as a pet. Usually the pet dragon would be of a very small variety, but some people had larger dragons as pets.

Siward, King of the Goths, had a daughter named Alfhild. When Alfhild was a little girl, Siward gave her a dragon egg. When it hatched, it turned out to be a poison spitting Orm. Siward was very protective of his daughter and when she became older he kept her locked in a room. Then, he decreed that if any man entered the room and failed to get past the dragon, he would be beheaded. Alfhild was then not bothered by any man and was kept safe.

In the country of Siword, prince Alf heard about King Siward and his daughter Alfhild. He liked a challenge and sailed to Gothland with the intention of wooing Alfhild.

As protection from the Orm's poison, he covered himself with a bloodstained hide. Alf killed the dragon and thought he had won the maiden.

Siward told Alf that Alfhild was to marry the man she chose of her own free will. Alfhild's mother did not like Alf and would not permit the wedding. Alfhild was not about to go against her mother and she became very depressed. She dressed like a man and ran away.

Alfhild joined a band of vikings and went raiding. Later Alf went in search of Alfhild. He eventually found her and the two were married.

5 THORA AND RAGNAR

Thora, the daughter of Herod Jarl in Gotland, had been given a dragon egg as a little girl. The baby dragon imprinted on Thora and followed her around as if she was its mother. As time went by, the dragon grew and became very protective of Thora.

After the dragon had killed some guards, Herod Jarl built a house for Thora some distance away from his mead hall.

The dragon, a poison spitting orm, would no longer let anyone near Thora. Herod built a shed where Thora with the dragon accompanying her could go and pick up food, water and a change of clothes. Thora now stayed in her house with the dragon. Eventually, the dragon became so big that it could no longer enter Thora's house. The dragon was so big that it lay coiled, completely surrounding the house. It now ate an ox each day.

Herod Jarl became concerned for his daughter and let it be, known that whoever would kill the dragon could have Thora for his wife. When Ragnar, the King of Denmark, heard about this, he sailed to Gotland. Ragnar dressed himself in skins covered with tar to protect himself from the dragon's poison. Then, he went to Thora's house with a spear and attacked the dragon and killed it.

After Ragnar had killed the dragon, the Jarl, Herod laughed at the sight of Ragnar and called him Lothbrok (Hairy pants). The name stuck and from that time on King Ragnar of Denmark was called Ragnar Lothbrok.

Herod Jarl held a wedding where Ragnar Lothbrok and Thora were married. The couple were deeply in love. They had three children, two boys and a daughter.

Thora Townhart, illustration by Jenny Nyström (1895)

6 SIGURD THE DRAGON SLAYER

Sigurd was a prince of the Volsungs. His father, King Sigmund died in battle before he was born. His mother, Hjordis, married King Alf who sent Sigurd to a tutor. The tutor told Sigurd about a dragon which had a huge horde of gold in a cave. The dragon, Fafnir, was a huge poison spitting Orm.

Sigurd's mother gave him his father's sword. This was a magic sword named Gram. There were magic swords in those days. Other examples of magic swords are Excalibur, King Arthur's sword and Tyrfing. The real "magic" of these swords was that they could cut through iron because they were made of steel.

Sigurd went to the cave of the dragon and observed the site. The Orm moved along the ground so there was a distinct path where it traveled in and out of the cave. In the evening, Sigurd saw the dragon go back into its lair.

During the night Sigurd used his sword to dig a pit in the middle of the downtrodden path. Then, he covered the pit with branches and leaves. Sigurd pushed some of the branches aside and went into the pit and recovered it with the branches and leaves. Then, he settled in to wait. He hoped that in this ambush he could avoid the dragon's poison.

In the morning the dragon came out of the cave to search for food. As it passed over the pit, Sigurd struck up with his sword and pierced the dragon's body.

Sigurd kept cutting away at the dragon until it died. Sigurd entered the dragon cave and there was indeed so much gold that now he was fabulously wealthy.

As Sigurd became established in the world, he met a woman named Brynhild. She was a Valkyrie. She was not one of Odin's mythical warrior women who collected the fallen warriors from the battle field. Women warriors were called shield maidens. A shield maiden who was exceptional as a warrior, and became famous for her deeds, was called a Valkyrie.

Brynhild and Sigurd fell in love and had personal relations which resulted in them having a daughter. They named the daughter Aslaug and she was fostered out to a man named Heimer. (In those days being fostered was different than it is today. Children were occasionally fostered out to someone that was known and trusted by the family. The purpose of this was to keep children safe and to teach the children various life skills). Eventually Aslaug married Ragnar Lothbrok.

7 THE CHURCH

The following are stories of dragons from the early church.

ST. BEATUS, HERMIT OF THUN, SWITZERLAND

Beatus was from either Ireland or Scotland. There are several accounts of this saint, so it depends on which story is read. Beatus was ordained and went to Rome. From there, he was sent with a companion, Achates, to evangelize the Helvetii.

Beatus and Achates set up camp in Argovia near the Ural Mountains. There, they converted many of the local people. From there, Beatus went south to the mountains above Lake Thun, near the village of Beatenburg and became a hermit. In the year 112 he decided to make a cave his home. However, when he entered the cave he encountered a dragon. Beatus fought the dragon and killed it.

The Church made Beatus a Saint. A monastery was built close to the cave which is now called St. Beatus caves.

SAINT QUIRINUS OF VAUX-SUR-SEINE, FRANCE

The Bishop Nicaseus was sent by Pope Clement to Gaul to help St. Denis to evangelize the inhabitants. Nicaeus was accompanied by Quirinus, a priest, and the deacon Scubiculus.

At Vaux-Sur-Seine they found that a dragon had laid waste to the area and had poisoned a well. On October 11, 285 Quirinus fought the dragon and killed it.

SAINT BIENHEURE OF VENDOME, FRANCE

Bienheure was a hermit. Before fighting a dragon he fasted and prayed. Then, he killed the dragon when it came to the river to drink.

SAINT LEONARD OF LIMOUSIN

Leonard was a Frankish nobleman who was baptized at the court of King Clovis in 498. He established a monastery at Noblac near Limoges where he became the abbot and led a religious life.

Leonard made a trip to England in the year 559. It was there that Leonard fought a dragon in a forest and killed it. Leonard was injured in his fight with the dragon. This was announced as the last dragon in England. However, in 1614 there were more dragon sightings.

The forest in which St. Leonard fought the dragon is now called St. Leonard's Forest. It is located 30 miles from London and 2 miles from Horsham.

Statue of St. Leonard's Forest Dragon

Photo by Horsham Photography used with permission.

Website:
https://horshamphotography.wordpress.com/2014/08/25/the
-dragon-in-st-leonards-forest/

SAINT GEORGE

George was a knight in the middle ages. A city was being plagued by a venom spitting dragon so the citizens began leaving offerings of sheep and cattle.

When they ran out of livestock to give the dragon they tried to appease it by offering it their children and youths. The children were chosen by holding a lottery.

St. George Slaying the Dragon - 1472-1 553

One day the king's daughter was chosen to be sacrificed to the dragon. However, George rescued the princess by killing the dragon.

With the death of the dragon the whole city was saved, and so it was that the church made him a Saint.

8 THE BIBLE

The Jews had been captured and taken to Babylon. There the King brought Daniel to a dragon and said to Daniel "You can not deny that this is a living god. So, worship him"

Daniel replied "I worship the Lord my God for He is the living God. But give me permission O King and I will kill this dragon without sword or club."

The King said "I give you permission."

Daniel took pitch, fat and hair and boiled them together. Of this he made cakes. He fed the cakes to the dragon. After the dragon ate the cakes, he burst open and died. Daniel said "See what you have been worshiping."

The people were angry that Daniel had killed the dragon and went to the King and demanded that Daniel be turned over to them. The King, surrounded by the angry mob, had no choice so he gave them Daniel. Then, the people threw Daniel into a den of lions.

There were seven lions. Every day the lions had been given two human bodies and two sheep. Now they were given nothing so that they would eat Daniel.

The prophet Habakkuk arrived with a stew and bread for Daniel which he ate while in the lion's den.

Daniel was in the lion's den for six days. On the seventh day the King came to the den of lions to mourn Daniel. He found Daniel alive and well, sitting there. Then, the King shouted "You are great O Lord of Daniel and there is no other God beside You."

The King pulled Daniel out and threw the people who had attempted Daniel's destruction into the den. They were immediately attacked by the lions and eaten.

Daniel 14:23-42

Babylonian Dragon – bas-relief mosaic on the Ishtar Gate

9 THE VIKINGS

The Vikings went out in their long ships to trade and raid from 800 A.D to 1050.

Viking Longboat

(Art work is "Viking Ship #13" from website: https://wallscover.com/viking-ship.html)

When going to a raid or to war, the vikings placed a carved dragon head on the high prow of their ships. This was to help to scare their opponents because people feared dragons.

The Norwegian King Olaf Tryggveson built the largest dragon ship known at that time. He named it "Ormen Den Lange". Translated to English: "The Long Dragon". Translators of his saga renamed it "The Long Serpent" because the translators did not believe in dragons. Other saga translators also translated orm or dragon as serpent or python. An example is the dragon fought by Ragnar Lothbrok was translated to "python". However, Scandinavia lies in the north where it is impossible for pythons to live in the wild.

Viking ship's dragon head – carved by Terry O'Sullivan

The Joms Vikings brought 60 ships to Jorund's Fjord to battle the army of Haakon Jarl who had brought 120 ships to the battle. The Joms Vikings lost after a tremendous sea battle. After the battle, several people reported seeing a sea serpent swim into Jorund's Fjord.

10 NORTHERN MYTHS AND LEGENDS

The greatest dragon of all was the Midgaard Serpent called Jordmungang. This dragon was so big that it surrounded the whole world and bit its own tail. Thor would try to kill the Midgard Serpent.

Thor left Asgaard and went on a trip. In the evening he reached the house of the Jotun, Hymir. Thor spent the night with Hymir. In the morning Hymir prepared to go deep sea fishing in a rowboat. Thor asked Hymir what they were taking as bait and Hymir told Thor to get his own bait. Thor looked around and saw Hymir's herd of oxen. He selected the biggest ox which was named Sky Bellower and struck off its head.

Thor took the ox head aboard the row boat and sat down in the stern. Hymir sat in the bow. Thor began to row the boat and Hymir thought that his row boat had never moved so fast before. They soon came to the place where Hymir was accustomed to sit and catch flat fish.

Thor said that he wanted to row farther out to sea. So, he rowed and the rowboat again went forward with great speed. They went so far out to sea that Hymir said it would be too dangerous to stay there because of the Midgaard Serpent. Thor said that he wanted to row out farther yet and he rowed a while more. Hymir was very displeased.

Finally Thor stopped rowing. He got out a very strong line, attached a huge and very strong hook, baited the hook with the ox head and threw it overboard.

Suddenly, the Midgaard Serpent snapped the ox head and the hook stuck in its mouth. The dragon jerked so hard that both Thor's fists struck the gunwale. Then, Thor grew angry and dug in both his heels. A powerful tug of war was going on.

The Midgard Serpent, Jordmungang, jerked hard on the line

Thor finally drew Jordmungang's head on board and stared straight at it. The dragon stared back and belched poison. The Jotun Hymir turned pale with fear. The giant dragon's head bobbed in and out of the boat with the thrashing of the waves. Thor drew back his hammer, Mjolnir, and took aim. Just then, Hymir in his fright, cut the line at the gunwale and the dragon disappeared under the ocean.

***Thor battling Jordmungang, the Midgaard Serpent by
Emil Doepler***

During the great world war called Ragnarok, Thor battled the
Midgaard Serpent. Thor managed to kill the dragon, but Thor
also died of the poison from the Midgaard Serpent.

BEOWULF

Beowulf was a prince in Jutland. A dragon was laying waste to the farm lands and killing people. Beowulf decided to kill it so, he gathered some warriors and went to the dragon's lair. When they saw the dragon, his men fled. Beowulf's friend, a Swede named Wiglaf, stayed with him. It was a fierce battle. When Beowulf was incapacitated, Wiglaf killed the dragon. Beowulf died soon after the battle.

Beowulf fighting the dragon.- 1908 illustration by J. R. Skelton

11 THE MIDDLE AGES

The church authorities announced that dragons were demons and should be destroyed. Saint George was not the only knight to kill a dragon. Many knights went in search of dragons. They went to known dragon caves, killed the dragons and became rich from the dragon's hoards.

The knights also killed dragons in forests and fields. These knights became famous and sometimes the King would give them a reward. Some dragon killers were made saints by the church. There were also unfortunate knights who killed a dragon and then soon after fell dead from the dragon's poison.

Sir Winkelried had been banished from his homeland because he had killed a man. When he heard that a dragon was terrorizing his community in his homeland, he offered to slay the dragon if he could get a pardon. The ruler took him up on it.

Sir Winkelried fixed a bundle of sharp spikes to his spear. Then, he found the dragon and attacked. He jammed the sharp spikes into the dragon's mouth, and he killed it with his sword. When the dragon was dead, the knight raised his sword high overhead in triumph and celebration. Blood on the sword ran down onto his exposed arm. The blood was so toxic that the knight died a short time after.

There was a dragon on the island of Rhodes, Greece. This dragon lived in a swamp. It was killing the cattle of the local farmers. Dieudonne de Gozon was the Grand Master of the Knights of Rhodes from 1346 to 1353. Gozon slew the dragon. He was then called by his nickname, "Dragon Slayer". Gozon took the head of the dragon and hung it on one of the seven gates of the Medieval town of Rhodes. The famous French scientist and traveler, Melchisedech Thevenot went to Rhodes to see the dragon's head for himself. He described the head as being larger than that of a horse with a huge mouth and teeth and large eyes. The head was on display until 1837. At that time it was disposed of by the workers responsible for fixing the gate.

By the end of the middle ages the dragons had been eradicated from Europe.

12 SOUTH AMERICA

In South America there was a huge dragon called the Feathered Serpent; a dragon with feathers. This dragon was worshiped. The Aztec and Toltecs called it Quetzialcotl. The Mayans called it Kukulkan. Temples and whole cities were built to worship this dragon. The best known place of worship was the pyramid of Kukulkan at Chichen-Itza in Mexico.

The pyramid of Kukulkan at Chichen-Itza in Mexico

MAJOR PERCY FAWCETT

Major Percy Fawcett surveyed the Amazon Basin for the Royal Geographical Society of London. In 1907 Major Fawcett and his Indian crew were drifting slowly down the Rio Abuna in a flimsy boat. Under their boat's bow there appeared a triangular head and several feet of undulating body. When the snake started to go up the bank, the Major shot it in the spine ten feet below the head. This caused a flurry of foam and several bumps against the boat's keel. The Major stepped ashore and measured the snake. 45 feet lay out of the water and 17 feet in it. When he came back to London, Percy Fawcett was branded a liar for claiming that he had bagged a 62 foot anaconda.

For over 100 years, explorers in the Amazon have claimed to have seen such huge anacondas. Cryptozoologist, Bernard Heuvelmans has verified these claims. It was not an anaconda. The snake was classified as titanoboa. It can reach a length of 150 feet and a weight of 5 tons.

FATHER VICTOR HEINZ

Father Victor Heinz was a missionary in South America. On May 22, 1922, Victor was being taken by a canoe on the Amazon from Brazil to his South American home. Suddenly he saw a giant water snake. Its body was as thick as an oil drum and it was 80 feet long. The boat men fell silent in fright. After they had passed far enough from the snake that the boat men dared to speak again, they said that the monster would have crushed us like matches if it had not just eaten several large capybaras (giant rodents).

FRANCISCO de AMARAL VARELLA

During the 1860's a worm like animal of gigantic size was seen in various parts of Brazil. Near the end of the 1860's Francisco de Amaral Varella saw something that looked like a huge earthworm on the banks of the Rio Caveiras. It was three feet thick and had a pig like snout on its head. When Francisco called out to his neighbours, the orm disappeared into the ground. In its wake it left deep furrows about 3 feet wide.

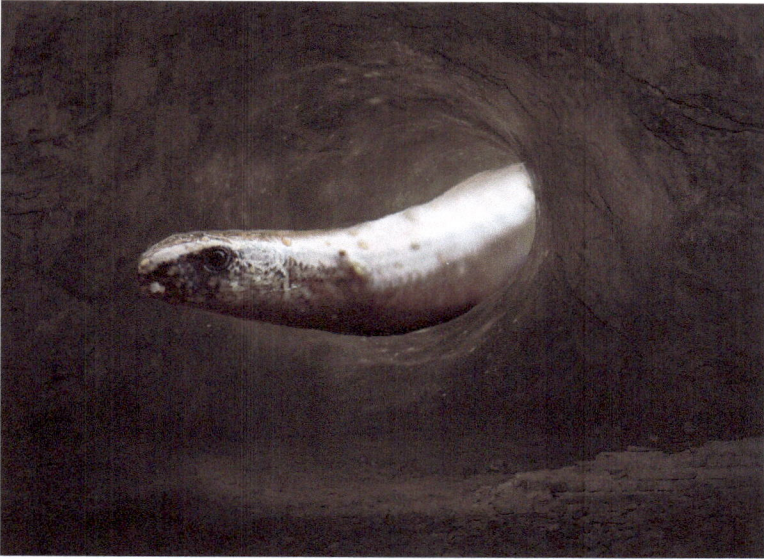

It looked like a huge earth worm three feet thick

13 CHINA

From 1271 to 1298, Marco Polo traveled in Asia, Persia, China, and Indonesia. He kept written records of his travels. These records are found in the book "The Travels of Marco Polo".

In the province of Karazan, China he observed dragons. Marco Polo wrote:

"They were 30 feet in length with a girth of about 8 feet. They had two short legs near the head. The paws had three claws like those of a tiger. The eyes were larger than a four penny loaf. The jaw was large enough to swallow a man and the teeth were large and sharp."

Other dragons described were 15 feet long. The dragons lurked in caves by day because of the heat. At night, they came out to find food.

The people hunted these dragons by placing wood covered with large spikes in the sand near drinking water, either streams or springs. The wood was placed so that only the spikes were above the sand. When a dragon came down to drink it was wounded by the spikes so that it was incapacitated. When a dragon was wounded, the crows in the area made a great noise which alerted hunters who came and finished the dragon off. The hunters skinned the dragon and took the meat. The dragon meat was considered a great delicacy and preferred to any other meat.

In ancient China people worshiped dragons. They believed dragons controlled the weather and other things in nature. During a particular dry period sometimes people would go to the mouth of a cave inhabited by a dragon. There they would kneel and pray for rain. People born in the year of the dragon were expected to accomplish great things in their lifetime.

Today, the Chinese still revere the dragon. The dragon dance is often performed during Chinese New Year.

A dragon parade during the dragon festival.

Another dragon parade

During the 5th day of the 5th lunar month each year, they hold a dragon boat festival.

Dragon Boat Race

14 MODERN SCIENCE

Dragon fossils have been around for a long time. Biologists like the Jesuit scholar, Athanasius Kirscher (1602 – 1680) have been describing them and classifying them.

Sir Richard Owen who was born in the beginning of the nineteenth century, became a palaeontologist and studied dragon fossils. Richard, who did not believe in dragons, said that they were the fossils of terrible lizards. In 1842 He put these fossils into their own taxonomic group and called them 'Dinosauria'. This classification was publicized all around the world and people were fascinated.

The dragons of Europe having been eradicated during the Middle Ages, and now being unrecognized by modern science, became just a creature of imagination and fiction found in myths and fairy tales. Thus it may be said that in 1842 dragons became dinosaurs.

Fossil Dinosaurs

Modern scientists have stated that the dinosaurs became extinct 65 million years ago. There were many theories about how the dinosaurs became extinct.

The first theory was that the first mammals hid in the daytime to escape from being eaten by the dinosaurs. These mammals were not like the mammals of today. They were all small creatures. It was stated that the dinosaurs being cold-blooded would become inactive at night therefore the early mammals were active at night. They would then come out of hiding and eat dinosaur eggs. Eventually this made the dinosaurs disappear. However, when it was later discovered that the dinosaurs were not cold-blooded, this theory had to be abandoned.

There was a theory that when the grasses became abundant, and eventually covered the world, the dinosaurs all caught hay fever which killed them off. This theory also died.

Another theory was that a nearby star went supernova. When the gamma radiation from this exploding star reached the earth, it killed the dinosaurs. Such gamma radiation from space hits the earth every 50 million years. However, this theory also died.

The theory at this time is that the mass extinction was caused by an asteroid or comet hitting the earth. Scientists found evidence of this object's strike near the town of Chicxulub in Mexico. This crater is 110 miles across. The object causing the crater would have to be six miles across. The explosion had the power of 100 trillion tons of TNT. This would be a billion times more force than the atomic bombs that hit Hiroshima and Nagasaki during the second world war.

The Chicxulub crater in Mexico

The result of this explosion would be dust in the atmosphere lasting for years which blocked the rays of the sun. The sun's rays being blocked caused winters which lasted for years. Then, the dust settled out of the atmosphere and came down with rain all over the earth. This changed ecological habitats. All this caused the extinction of many species. The extinctions took place over many years; probably at least 10,000 years or more which is just a blink of an eye in geological time.

Not just dinosaurs became extinct from this comet or asteroid strike. Many other animals became extinct as well. But not all dinosaurs became extinct from this event.

15 DRAGONS OF TODAY

In Texas, fossil dinosaur tracks and human tracks are found in the riverbed of the Paluxy River, near Glen Rose. In one case a human footprint overlapped that of a three toed dinosaur.

In May 2012, a triceratops brow horn was discovered in Dawson county, Montana. It was found by paleontologist Otis Kline Jr., microscope scientist, Mark Armitage, and microbiologist and paleontologist, Kevin Anderson. The horn was subjected to C-14 dating and was found to be 35,000 years old.

The Columbus Dispatch published an article on November 3, 1991. It stated that Soviet scientists confirmed that dinosaurs and humans were contemporaries as recently as 10,000 years ago. Soviet scientists Dmitri Kouznetsov and Andrey Ivanov said tests showed many dinosaur bones were 9,800 to 30,000 years old.

16 LOCH NESS

Not all the dragons of Europe had been exterminated. The knights were unable to go into the water to kill the water dragons and sea serpents.

Stories of a water dragon in Loch Ness go back 1,500 years. Saint Adaman's biography from 700 A.D. tells a story from 565 or 580. The story has Saint Colomba facing a dragon on the River Ness. The dragon was aggressive but Saint Colomba caused the dragon to flee backwards faster than it had approached. There is also a story of Vikings seeing the Loch Ness monster.

There were sightings reported back to the middle of the nineteenth century. Most reports described the creature as a large animal, the back as black or gray resembling an overturned boat. The large animal had a long thin neck and a small head which was somewhat like a horse. On some occasions the long tapered body would be seen with flipper like appendages and a thick extended tail.

A small insignificant story of the monster was reported in the Inverness paper, the Northern Chronicle on August 27, 1930.

On April 14, 1933, Mr. and Mrs. John Mackay of Drumnadrochit stopped their car to watch an enormous animal rolling and plunging in the water. In May, 1933 the story of the strange occurrence was run in the newspaper, the Inverness Courier. The newspaper called the creature a monster. A follow up story by the paper was headlined, "Loch Ness Monster".

On July 22, 1933, Mr. and Mrs. George Spicer on vacation, were driving on a road running by Loch Ness. About 200 yards ahead the bracken on a hillside suddenly became agitated. From the bracken suddenly emerged a long necked animal. It moved jerkily across the narrow road. George stepped on the gas to get a closer look. But the animal had lumbered through the bushes on the Loch side and disappeared.

One year later there had been 20 more sightings and the creature was named Nessie.

A sighting of Nessie

On January 5, 1934, Arthur Grant was driving his motorcycle fast along the Loch road near Lochend. It was a bright moonlit night. Arthur saw a large, dark, blob shadowed by the bushes along the road ahead. As he approached, the creature bounded across the road almost colliding with Arthur's motorcycle. In the moonlight Grant saw a creature with a small eel like head with oval eyes. It had a long neck and a bulky body thickening toward a long rounded off tail. It had four flipper-like legs. The animal was dark colour and he estimated it to be 18 to 20 feet long. Arthur jumped off his motorcycle and pursued the animal which loped away fast and disappeared into the Loch with a splash.

Robert T. Gould, a chronicler, stated he thought that Nessie was a single stranded sea serpent. But in order to survive there had to be a family of Nessies. On July 14, 1937, there was reported a sighting of three monsters about 300 yards out in the Loch. There were two shiny black humps, 5 feet long and protruding 2 feet out of the water and on either side, a smaller Nessie.

In September 1997, Michael Thompson Noel, a reporter for London's Financial Times, wrote that he had seen 5 Nessies bobbing side by side. They were greenish-brown and had three or four humps. One was a small juvenile. The animals ranged in size from 3 to 65 feet. Most people who have sighted Nessie estimated their size to be from 15 to 30 feet.

People came to Loch Ness to study Nessie. Sonar has tracked moving animals underwater such as schools of fish. However some were obviously not fish but quite large animals. A picture of a large fin was captured from a submarine.

On April 23, 1960, Tim Dinsdale was on a watch over Loch Ness. Looking through binoculars he spotted a large oval shape well above the water. It had a distinct mahogany colour. When it started to move, he realized it was an animal. He took 4 minutes of film before it submerged. Many other video tapes and photos have been taken after 1960.

On May 24, 2018, the Toronto Sun newspaper ran an article that announced that a New Zealand scientist, Neil Gemmell, would be leading an international team to the lake in June of 2018 to conduct DNA tests on water samples to determine what species live there. When creatures moves about in the water they leave behind fragments of DNA that come from their urine, scales, skin and other such parts of the body.

They will take 300 samples from different parts of the lake. Then, they will filter the organic material and extract the DNA, sequencing it by using technology originally created for the human genome project. The DNA results will then be compared against a database of known species. They should have answers by the end of the year 2018 (sometime after the publication of this book).

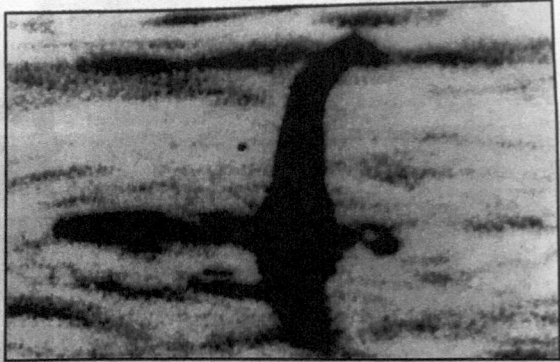

The Toronto Sun ■ THURSDAY, MAY 24, 2018

Using DNA to search for Loch Ness Monster

WELLINGTON, New Zealand — The stories seem as tall as the lake is deep.

For hundreds of years, visitors to Scotland's Loch Ness have described seeing a monster that some believe lurks in the depths.

But now the legend of "Nessie" may have no place left to hide.

A New Zealand scientist is leading an international team to the lake next month, where it will take samples of the murky waters and conduct DNA tests to determine what species live there.

University of Otago professor Neil Gemmell says he's no believer in Nessie, but he wants to take people on an adventure and communicate some science along the way.

Besides, he says, his kids think it's one of the coolest things he's ever done.

One of the more far-fetched theories is that Nessie is a long-necked plesiosaur that some-how survived the period when dinosaurs became extinct.

Another theory is that the monster is actually a sturgeon or giant catfish.

Many believe the sightings are hoaxes or can be explained by floating logs or strong winds.

Gemmell said that when creatures move about in water, they leave behind tiny fragments of DNA.

It comes from their skin, feathers, scales and urine.

He said his team will take 300 samples of water from different points around the lake and at different depths.

— The Associated Press

The most famous photo of "Nessie," the monster many believe lives in the depths of Scotland's murky Loch Ness. *AP FILES*

Newspaper article from the Toronto Sun on May 24, 2018

17 CRYPTOZOOLOGY

The biologists studying Nessie and other unknown monsters are known as crypto zoologists. They are ridiculed by main stream scientists. These brave biologists hunt unknown monsters all over the world. Loren Coleman and Patrick Huyghe wrote the book "The Field Guide To Lake Monsters, Sea Serpents, And Other Mystery Denizens Of The Deep". In an appendix they have a list of Lake and River Monsters World Wide. Such a list of monsters is also found on Wikipedia.

https://en.wikipedia.org/wiki/List_of_reported_lake_monsters

The Academy of Applied Science sent an expedition to Loch Ness in June, 1975. They had a camera-strobe system and a sonar system. The main camera system was to be triggered by the sonar. It was placed on a bottom ledge at a depth of 80 feet. The back up camera strobe was suspended from a boat at a level of 40 feet above the primary system.

Many times the sonar record showed large objects near the sophisticated camera. But the film revealed nothing because the bottom had been stirred up so that clouds of silt surrounded the camera. There were excellent shots of the silt cloud.

The back up camera at 40 feet functioned perfectly. It took pictures for 24 hours from June 19 to June 20. Several pictures showed large objects within the strobe light beam. One picture showed portions of a pinkish body. Another picture showed the upper torso, neck, and head of a living creature with two stubby appendages. There were also pictures of eels and fish. One sequence of frames showed that the camera had been disturbed and set in a slow rocking motion ending up to show the bottom of the boat. Then, the next frame showed the head of a dragon facing the camera. The face showed nostrils, an open mouth, and several horn-like projections. A study of these pictures was used to calculate that the living creature had a length of 20 feet, a neck about one and a half feet thick, a mouth 9 inches long and 5 inches wide, and horns about 6 inches long set about 10 inches apart. This was only one specimen. It was concluded that other specimens could be considerably bigger.

The living creature had a length of 20 feet (Artwork by Heinrich Harder 1858 - 1935)

On July 8, 1975, Allen Wilkins and his son, Ian, were about one and a half miles south of Invermoriston. At 7:20 a.m. Wilkins saw a 20 foot long black shape appear and disappear some distance down the Loch. At 10:12 a.m. Wilkins, his wife, and several other people watched and photographed three large triangular humps playfully moving about in the water. The humps vanished when a motor boat appeared.

On July 12, 1976, two Inverness mechanics were in a boat about a quarter mile off Abriachan Pier. When they saw a hump trailing in their wake, they slowed down and turned the boat around and headed back for a closer look. Then, five humps were weaving and bobbing around them. The humps were 10 to 12 feet long and 2 to 3 feet high. The two men put on their life jackets and held onto the boat. They watched the animals for about 15 minutes. Then, a rainstorm came and the men started shoreward. They were followed for a while by one of the animals.

In March 2002, Bobbie Pollock, a post man from Glasgow, released to the media a three and a half minute video of an unidentified black creature rising five feet out of the water of Loch Ness. He had shot the video in August 2000. He had held off releasing it because he had feared ridicule. Just as he had surmised, he did receive a lot of ridicule after he released the video.

18 OGOPOGO

Okanagan Lake in British Columbia is connected to the Pacific Ocean by the Columbia River. A huge aquatic creature has been reported seen in the lake about 100 times since the year 1700. Just like at Loch Ness, people come to Okanagan Lake to see the creature. Over the years, the creature has become affectionately known as "Ogopogo". Many people have spent several days staring at the water of the lake without seeing the creature.

On July 2, 1949, Mr. Leslie L. Kerry of Kelowna took the W. F. Watson family of Montreal on a boat ride. They spotted a large snake like form in the water. The creature was about 30 feet long and about a foot in diameter. The creature undulated in the water sometimes travelling on top of the water and sometimes below the water. It had a forked tail that lashed up and down. The group watched Ogopogo for longer than 15 minutes.

Mrs. Kerry saw Ogopogo from shore and called her neighbours, Dr. and Mrs. Stanley Underhill. They watched the event with binoculars. Dr. Underhill said that it was smooth and black. He thought that there were two creatures because of the distance between some of the undulating coils which he estimated as being about seven feet long.

On July 17, 1959, Mr. R.H. Miller and his wife were on their way home in their motor cruiser. In their cruiser were also their friends. Mr. and Mrs. Pat Marten and their son, Murray. Miller noticed a large creature following in their boat's wake at a distance of about 250 feet. Marten turned the boat to get a better look. They slowly moved closer and watched Ogopogo through binoculars. It had a blunt nosed snake like head. As they approached, the creature gradually submerged and disappeared.

On July 23, 1968, five water skiers aged 14 to 21 were skiing across Okanagan Lake. One of the skiers, Sheri Campbell, saw a 20 foot creature floating lazily on the surface of the water. She was so startled that she let go of the tow-rope. After she had been treading water for a few minutes, her friends picked her up. The group decided to follow Ogopogo. They got within 5 feet of it and saw its blue-green-grey scales glittering in the sun. Then, Ogopogo submerged and swam off leaving a wake of V shaped waves. The young skiers chased it at a speed of 40 miles per hour. The boat soon fell behind and the skiers lost sight of Ogopogo.

19 LAKE CHAMPLAIN

There are many lakes around the world where monsters have been sighted, such as Ogopogo in Okanagan Lake and Cressie in Newfoundland's Crescent Lake. Lake Champlain is another lake such as these.

Lake Champlain lies on the border between Vermont and New York. Over the years, hundreds of people have seen the Lake Champlain monster. It has been named "Champ".

In 1977 Sandra Mansi took a picture of Champ. She said that the neck stood six feet out of the water and that the body was about 12 feet long. The animal floated motionless for about 4 or 7 minutes and then submerged.

Champ

20 TROUT LAKE, ONTARIO

Trout Lake is a deep, cold water lake near North Bay, Ontario from which North Bay draws its drinking water. Trout Lake has its very own Trout Lake Monster. Stories of the Trout Lake Monster go very far back in time. People have seen large swells of water, shadows, and figures of varied proportions and sizes. The local newspaper, "The North Bay Nugget" ran a story in the 1970's about the Trout Lake Monster which included a picture of people staring at the water hoping to catch sight of the Trout Lake Monster.

On May 25, 1956, Margaret and Allan Campbell after eating lunch, went with their dog out on the lake in their fiber glass boat. They were never seen again. Whether it had anything to do with the monster or not, this event became part of the Trout Lake Monster stories.

In 2006, the Ontario Provincial Police received a tip from a recreational fisherman. Using high tech imaging equipment, they found the bodies of the Campbells at the bottom of the lake, not far from their cottage. Their boat was also found nearby at the bottom of the lake. A local resident, while swimming at Camp Island, found a large tooth. He brought the tooth to the Ministry of Natural Resources. The Ministry of Natural Resources destroyed the tooth. The people who knew about the tooth thought that this was a conspiracy theory.

Because of the stories of the Trout Lake Monster, a local band named themselves "The Trout Lake Monster". They played in the 1970's and 1980's.

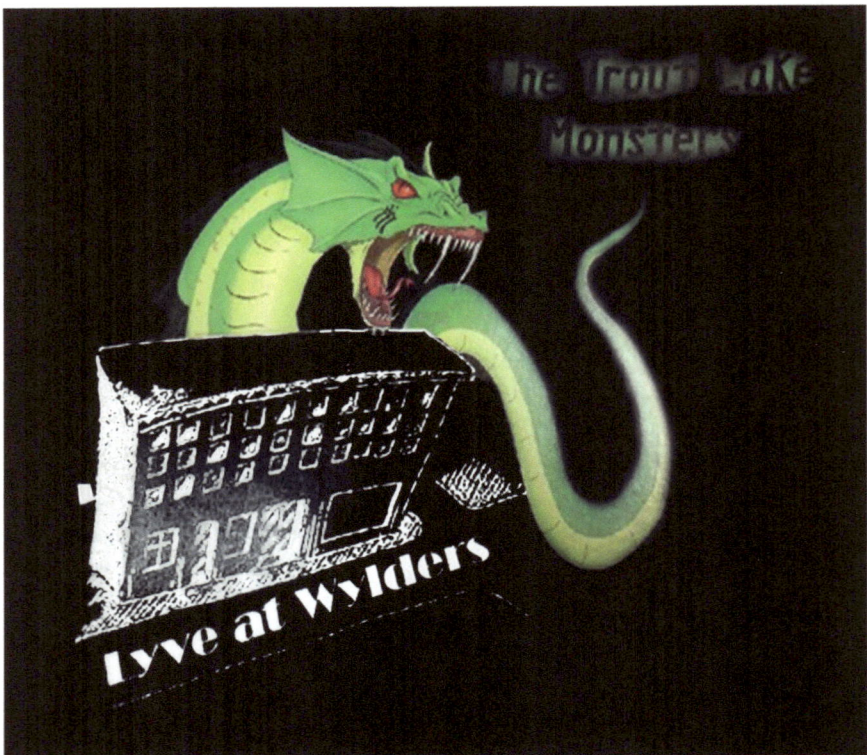

CD cover for local band called The Trout Lake Monster

21 CLASSIFICATION OF LAKE MONSTERS

Encounters with lake monsters like Nessie, Ogopogo, and Champ are rare. Loren Coleman and Patrick Huyghe have described 14 types in their field guide called "The Field Guide To Lake Monsters, Sea Serpents And Other Mystery Denziens Of The Deep". These animals are elusive and intelligent, therefore, they are not likely to allow themselves to get caught.

There are lake monsters found all over the world. They are usually called lake monsters except for the creatures which are obviously of the same species. Nessie is a local name and other local names are used in different areas and countries. This is because they have not been classified scientifically so they are called monsters. Many lake monsters seem to be the same species as Nessie.

In British Columbia there are the Ogopogo species in Kamloops Lake, Kathlyn Lake, Kootenay Lake, Lower Arrow Lake, Martin's Lake, Moberly Lake, Okanagan Lake, Osoyoos Lake, Skaha Lake, and Williams Lake. Other lakes in British Columbia also have a lake monster with a different name. Two examples are Tag at Tagai Lake, and Shuswaggi at Shuswap Lake.

In Alberta, the Ogopogo species is found in Battle River, Bow River, Clearwater River; and in South Saskatchewan River there is an Agopogo.

In Peter Pond River in Saskatchewan is found a water dragon named Puff.

In Manitoba, both Lake Winnipeg and Lake Winnipegosis have Winnipogo.

Ontario has many lakes where the water dragon is simply called "monster". However, Muskrat Lake has Mussie, Nith River has Slimy Casper, Lake Ontario has Kingstie, and Oshawa has Oscar. Lake Simcoe has Igopogo, Lake Temiscaming has Mugwump and Thunder Bay has Merbeing.

Quebec has many lake dragons. Most of these dragons are known only as "monster". However, Lac Decaire has Lizzie, Lac Memphremagog has Memphre and Lac Pohenegamook has Ponik.

In Nova Scotia, Beathac mor Loch Ainaslaigh is found in Lake Ainslie.

In Newfoundland, Crescent Lake has Cressie. Swanger's Cove has a water dragon called Maggot.

Scientific classification of these water monsters is impossible without samples. Obviously DNA testing has been impossible.

The Nessies are found all over the world. With so many Nessies it is amazing that no one has made a thorough scientific study. The cryptozoologists are trying very hard. When I worked as a fisheries biologist I found it very easy to obtain samples of fish to study. However, the cryptids are very intelligent and very elusive. It is very hard to even catch a sight of one.

22 SEA SERPENTS

Stories of sea serpents are found in all cultures which have contact with the sea. When I was in university, one of my biology professors assured his class that sea serpents were real. He talked about some biologists who went diving into the Pacific Ocean just out from Victoria Island in British Columbia. There they saw a sea serpent.

In September 1959, Tex Geddes, a basking shark fisherman, and James Gavin, an engineer, went out in Geddes's boat. They set out from the coast of Soay, an island famous for sheep, just off the west coast of Scotland.

They saw a large dark object approach their boat. When it came closer they saw a large, humped-back, scaly, creature with a prominently serrated back. It had a rounded tortoise-like head, with a large mouth which it kept opening and closing. Then, they heard it breathe through its mouth. The part of its body that was exposed to the air, was between 8 and 10 feet in length. The size of the head was compared to that of a donkey.

Left: A drawing of the sea serpent made by Tex Geddes
Right: A drawing of the same creature by James Gavin

The Illustrated London News ran a story about the event. Geddes wrote to zoologist Maurice Burton about the encounter.

An artists sketch of Geddes' sea dragon in their local newspaper

There are many stories from early sailors about sea serpents seen undulating in the water. If a sailor got too close, he would be eaten.

Olaus Magnus was a Catholic Priest who was exiled from his homeland in Sweden. He wrote about a sea serpent he had seen in 1522 near an island called Moo in the Diocese of Hammer. The sea dragon was about 75 feet long.

Olaus saw more than just the one sea serpent. The most notorious was a serpent over 200 feet long with a black body 20 feet thick. It had hair hanging from its neck (a cubit long). It had flaming, shiny eyes. It lived in rocks and caves. A drawing of this serpent shows it coiled around a Norman ship eating one of the crew members.

Sea Serpent from Olaus Magnus woodcut illustration in 'History of the Nordic Peoples' (from 1555)

In 1639, a sea serpent was spotted off the coast of New England near Cape Ann, Massachusetts. It was given the name Gloucester's Sea Serpent. It was named after a harbour just north of Boston. The serpent was about 90 feet long.

Hans Poulsen Egede, a Danish, Norwegian Lutheran did missionary work in Greenland. There he observed a sea serpent off the coast on July 6, 1734.

In 1746, Captain de Ferry had been on a sea voyage. Off the coast of Norway his men became excited, yelling that there was a sea serpent in the water. The captain rushed on deck. The creature had a head which was raised about two feet out of the water. It resembled the head of a horse but the mouth was quite large. It had black eyes and a long white mane hanging down into the water. There were 7 or 8 coils of the serpent's body which was a greyish colour. The body undulated in an up and down manner which is impossible for snakes.

Reports of sea serpents continued for hundreds of years. In 1818 James Prince, marshal of the district of Nahant, sighted a sea serpent seven times. The sea dragon was about 50 feet in length. The dragon submerged and reemerged at roughly eight minute intervals. Thus Prince concluded that the creature needed to breathe air.

On July 15, 1825, a gentleman reported a sea serpent sighting in the harbour of Halifax, Nova Scotia. The serpent moved by a wriggling sort of motion. It was about 60 feet long and about 180 feet from shore.

On May 15, 1883, several members of the British Army and two members of the Royal Navy were on a boat heading for a popular fishing spot somewhere between St. Margaret's Bay and Mahone Bay. The men got bored and started to take pot shots at some grampuses (dolphins or other toothed whales, such as the orca). Suddenly the head and neck of a denizen of the deep, looking like that of a snake, rose out of the water. The head was about 6 feet long and its body was about 100 feet long. The width of the neck was about the size of a modest sized tree.

On August 6, 1848, the HMS Daedalus was traveling to St. Helena. When it was between the Cape of Good Hope and St.Helena many well respected citizens of society saw a sea serpent. The head remained about 4 feet from the water and the visible body measured about 60 feet or more. The colour was dark brown with whitish areas at the throat. It had a mane covering its head.

In 1876, Captain George Drevar of the barque, Paoline, saw a whale fighting a sea serpent off the north-east coast of Brazil.

On July 19, 1879, Captain Davidson of the steam ship Kiushiro-maru was about 14 kilometers from the shore of Cape Satano at the island of Kiu Siu, Japan. A whale jumped clear out of the sea about 1,300 feet from the ship. There was something holding onto the belly of the whale. The whale made another jump. Then, a serpent creature rose about 30 feet out of the water. The serpent was as thick as a junk's mast. After standing a few seconds in an upright position, the serpent descended back under the water.

A sea serpent inhabiting the North American Pacific coast has been sighted since 1892. In 1933 Archie Wills, editor of the Victoria Times sponsored a "name that creature contest". The winning name was "Cadborosaurus" (from Cadboro Bay in Greater Victoria). This was eventually shortened to Caddy. This sea serpent is long and thin with several humps. The head is horse-like with a mane or crest.

On Halloween in 1983, construction workers were repairing a California highway. From the cliff overlooking Stinson Beach north of San Francisco they saw a huge black monster that rose to a height of ten feet above the water. Its mouth was four feet wide. The body was about 60 feet long. Five construction workers reported seeing this sea serpent. The New York Times reported the story and also presented another sighting which had occurred on April 5, 1885.

The number of sea serpent sightings have declined over the years. One reason for this is the ridicule factor. People do not like to be ridiculed. Another reason is that there are fewer boats on the oceans now. The boats plying the waters now are noisy which tends to keep marine life of all kinds away.

People now travel in ocean liners and cruise ships. These ships travel in well-established shipping lanes which marine life tend to avoid. The best way to see marine life is on a silent vessel.

The Norwegian explorer, Thor Heyerdal, and his friends Knud Haugland, Torstein Raaby, Erik Hesselberg, Herman Watzinger, and a Swede, Bendt Danielsson, built a raft in Peru out of 45 foot Balsa logs. They named the raft "Kon Tiki" and set sail on April 28, 1947. They sailed the raft for 101 days and covered 4,300 miles across the Pacific Ocean. On August 7, 1947, the raft crashed into a reef at Raroia in the Tuamotus. They made a successful landing.

The raft Kon Tiki, 1947

While at sea, the crew saw many rare sea creatures. Several unidentified animals were also observed. In the ship's log one is described as a "thick dark-coloured fish with a broad white body, thin tail, and spikes". Another was described as "a six foot long creature that wiggled its body like an eel, had a thin snout, large dorsal fin near the head and a smaller one in the middle of the back, as well as a heavy sickle-like tail fin".

On several occasions, the raft passed "a huge dark mass the size of the floor of a room".

A huge dark mass the size of the floor of a room

One night " three huge phosphorescent forms circled the raft for hours without surfacing" The crew assumed they were backs of animals. The visible portions measured 30 feet long.

23 KOMODO DRAGON

The Komodo dragon is a monitor lizard that grows to a maximum length of 10 feet. It is found on the Indonesian islands of Komodo, Rinca, Flores, Gill Motang, and Padar which lie between Java and Australia. Sometimes large dragons enter the ocean and swim to nearby islands to hunt.

The dragon is carnivorous and its bite is poisonous. The dragon bites its prey and when the prey runs away or walks away, the Komodo dragon follows it until the prey dies of the poison. Then, the dragon eats the prey. They eat large prey such as water buffalo, deer, pigs, young Komodo Dragons, and humans. The young dragons live in trees where they are safe from predators including cannibalistic Komodo Dragons.

Five people killed by a Komodo Dragon took place in 1974, 2000, 2007, and 2009. During that time there have been at least eight other people injured by them.

In 2007 a Dragon killed a fisherman. The same year a young boy, about 8 years old, was on a beach. He had to urinate and went to the bushes and stepped behind a tree. There, lying in ambush, was a Dragon. The Dragon killed him.

On May 4, 2017, Lon Lee Allee, a tourist from Singapore, was on a trip to Indonesia. In West Manggarrai he refused to pay a tour guide and went out alone. He entered a secluded area to watch Komodo Dragons feed on goats and pigs. People in the area warned him not to get too close. Lon ignored the warnings and crept up on one dragon to take pictures.

The 8 foot long dragon attacked him. The onlookers rushed over and dragged him away. Lon was first treated on the island and then taken by boat to Siloam General Hospital. A tour guide said that it was the first incident of a human being bitten in the past 5 years.

Many zoos now keep Komodo dragons. Some of these are: San Diego Zoo, Toronto Zoo, Smithsonian's National Zoo, Denver Zoo, Atlanta Zoo, Calgary Zoo, Taronga Zoo, Minnesota Zoo, Houston Zoo, Perth Zoo, Akron Zoo, and the Barcelona Zoo.

The Komodo Dragon is poisonous

Komodo National Park has an area of 700 square miles. Main, a 46 year old Ranger was doing paper work at his desk when a Komodo Dragon slithered up the stairs of Main's wooden hut. The dragon latched on to Main's ankle which was dangling beneath the desk. Main tried to pry open the dragon's jaws but the dragon sank its teeth into his hand. Other rangers heard Main's screams and came to his rescue. Main was rushed to the hospital where he received 55 stitches. Three months later his hand and ankle were still swollen.

24 MOKELE MBEMBE

In Africa, the People's Republic of the Congo, is a vast hot, humid area covered with thick forests containing many streams and swamps. One of these swamps is the largest swampland in the world, the Likouala Swamp. It has an area of 55,000 square miles. It is larger than the state of Florida. The government has declared that it is 80% unexplored. The scientific community regards it as alien; as if it were an entirely new planet.

In 1776, French missionaries saw huge footprints on the forest floor. The footprints were 3 feet in diameter with three claw marks. The prints were spaced about 7 feet apart. The local people said that the tracks were not from elephants and elephants do not have claws. They said that the tracks belonged to a different animal. The natives called the animal Mokele Mbembe. One of the priests saw several of the animals that belonged to these tracks, chewing on vegetation while wading in a river.

Track of the Mokele Mbembe

Expeditions looking for Mokele Mbembe began in the 1880's shortly after the region had been taken over by Belgium.

In 1913, a German explorer reported stories told by the local people. Scientists, from descriptions of the animal, said that it sounded like it was a sauropod dinosaur. Sauropods were the giants of the dinosaur world. They averaged about 70 feet long and stood 12 to 15 feet tall at the hips.

Mokele Mbembe (Brontosaurus)

In 1932, a British scientist who was exploring near the Likouala region came across some abnormally huge footprints. Later, he went down one of the rivers in a canoe. He heard strange sounds but did not see anything.

Also, in 1932, the world-famous zoologist, Ivan T. Sanderson and animal trader, Gerald Russel paddled up the Mainuy River. Sanderson's report stated as follows: "The most terrifying sound I have ever heard, which sounded like an oncoming earthquake or a nearby exploding robot, suddenly greeted us from a large underwater cave."

The water of the river was boiling and foaming directly in front of their canoe. Suddenly a darkish shiny lizard-like head emerged from the water. The head was the size of a fully grown hippo's head. The head sat on a thick swan-like neck. The neck turned and the creature stared at Sanderson and Russel for a few seconds. Sanderson said later, that it seemed like an eternity. The two men were terrified.

In 1980 and 1981, biologist Roy Mackal headed expeditions into the Likouala and Lake Tele regions of the Congo. They never saw the dragon but they gathered many stories about it from the natives. Mokele Mbembe is a herbivore. It eats foliage from trees and reaches higher in trees for foliage than a giraffe can. Mokele Mbembe hates crocodiles and hippopotamus which they kill when they run across one. Strangely, this area of the lowlands has an unusually low hippo population.

Mokele Mbembe hates hippopotamus

Mokele Mbembe live in caves of the river bank which they dig out. They are not seen in the dry season because they hide out in their caves.

In 1980, engineer Herman Regusters and his wife Kia mounted an expedition to Lake Tele. They heard growls and roars of an unknown creature. Then, they watched it walking on land. It was 30 to 35 feet long. Eventually they saw it and took pictures of it in the lake (albeit, grainy and unclear pictures). They also returned with plaster prints, sound recordings, and samples of droppings. The sound recordings were subjected to technical evaluation with a zoological source noted, but were not conclusive except noting that the sounds were not attributable to known wildlife.

Herman Regusters photo of Mokele Mbembe

Dinosaur-Like Beast Photographed During African Jungle Expedition

LOS ANGELES (AP) — Dinosaur hunter Herman Regusters and his wife, Kia, returned to California yesterday with photographs they hope will prove the existence of a modern dinosaur, an associate said.

"They were taking a lot of photographs in the Congo and at one point they said they possibly got a photo of the creature but it was very difficult conditions," John Sack, a friend of Regusters who has handled details of the expedition in the United States, said in a telephone interview.

"The creature was just poking its head out of the water and diving back in. The photo was not developed in the Congo, of course, but will be developed very carefully at Jet Propulsion Laboratory (in Pasadena), where Herman worked," Sacks said. "Nobody knows now what's on the photograph."

The photographs will be shown Tuesday at a news conference to be held by the Regusters, Sack said.

Regusters, a 47-year-old consulting engineer, left for the Congo in September. He spent several weeks in its capital city of Brazzaville before taking his party about 500 miles farther into the jungle to the Lake Tele area, where most of the sightings of "mokele-mbembe" have been reported.

Regusters said before leaving that natives have long reported sighting the creature, thought possibly to be a survivor of a dinosaur species believed extinct for 60 million years.

The creature was "dark brownish in color, the skin appeared slick and smooth, with a long neck and small head," Sack reported. "Because of the long neck, it was not a hippo or elephant. It was no animal known to any of the people on the expedition."

Sacks said the couple had endured difficult conditions in seeking the creature and that Regusters had lost 32 pounds.

Many members of the expedition had seen the creature and heard it making noise, he said.

"Herman saw it. Kia saw it and they saw it on several occasions and they heard it making this tremendous roar," he said. "Many other members of the expedition, and this includes government officials from the Republic of the Congo, saw it and heard it. It's not just two people from Pasadena who have seen it. It's a number of people."

Testimony of Herman & Kia Regusters' trip to the Congo.

In 1983, a Congolese expedition was led by Marcellin Agnagna, a biologist with the Brazzaville Zoo. They saw Mokele Mbembe out in Lake Tele. The animal was watching them.

In 1987, a Japanese film crew filmed Mokele Mbembe in the lake. The film was of poor quality.

In 2000, two Congolese security guards saw Mokele Mbembe in Boumba River, Cameroon.

One story, told by the natives, was that a young boy went canoeing on the river. He rounded a bend in the river and came face to face with Mokele Mbembe. He quickly turned his canoe around and paddled as fast as he could back to his village.

Another story was told about villagers attacking and killing a Mokele Mbembe. The villagers cut the meat up and took it back to the village. There, the villagers had a big feast.

The villagers killed a Mokele Mbembe

A few days later the village was attacked by a herd of Mokele Mbembe. All the villagers were killed and the village was destroyed.

The village was attacked by a herd of Mokele Mbembe

Cryptozoologists have stated that the Babylonian dragon which was killed by Daniel was probably a Mokele Mbembe. They conjecture that it was captured as a baby either in the Congo or Cameroon and transported to Babylon.

There was a movie made about Mokele Mbembe. The movie was released on March 22, 1985. The title was "Baby: Secret of the Lost Legend". The stars were Patrick McGoohan and Sean Young. The short plot: "A paleontologist and her husband discover a baby Brontosaurus and its mother in Africa, and try to protect them from a group of hunters intent on capturing the dinosaurs."

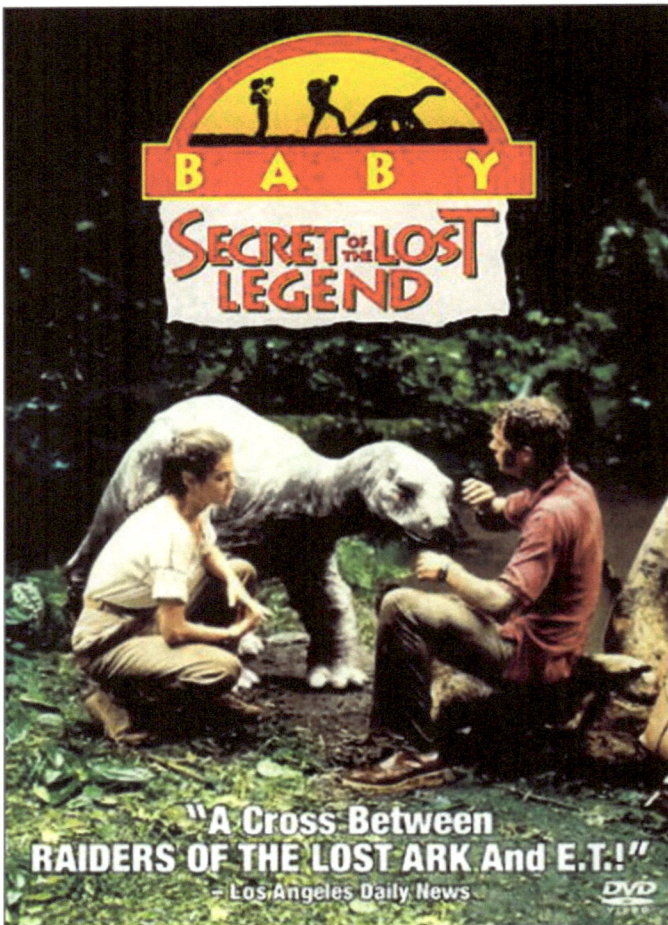

DVD cover for the movie Baby: Secret Of The Lost Legend

25 AFRICAN DRAGONS

Mokele Mbembe is not the only dragon in Africa.

EMELA-NTOUKA

In 1981, cryptozoologist, Professor Roy P. Mackal, found a swamp monster in the Belgian Congo. In the Likoula swamp lands his team found a creature called Emela-Ntouka which is native for 'Killer of Elephants'. It is semi-aquatic and the size of an elephant. It has a long heavy tail, four sturdy legs, and one long, very sharp, horn on its snout.

Roy Mackal's drawing of the Emela-ntouka
(Mackal, Roy, A Living Dinosaur, 1987, p. 236)

Emela-ntouka is a herbivore. However, it has a nasty disposition. If an elephant or buffalo enters the lake where it lives, it will attack the intruder and stab it with its long, sharp, horn. It will disembowel the elephant or buffalo. It is a ceratopsian or horned dinosaur. Another member of the ceratopsians is the triceratops.

NGOUBOU

In November 2000, William Gibbons and David Woetzel were exploring in the Savanna region of Cameroon. The pygmies told them about Ngoubou. That name is translated as Rhinoceros. However, the pygmies said that it was no ordinary rhinoceros and that it had more than one horn. They also stated that the father of one of the pygmies had killed a Ngoubu a number of years ago.

A railroad construction worker had reported seeing a Ngoubu on November 17, 1919.

Gibbons, himself, found a Ngoubu and had to flee when it charged. He had discharged his rifle at it with no effect.

NGUMA-MONENE

The first sighting of Nguma-Monene was in 1961 near the Dongu Mataba, a tributary of the Ubangi River in the Republic of the Congo. In 1971, pastor Joseph Ellis described the animal as 35 feet long and brown in colour. On its back were diamond shaped ridges. It had a low slung body.

Biologist, Roy P. Mackal, led two expeditions into the Likouala swamps. He described the animal as having a low slung body and that it never raised itself after leaving the water. The local inhabitants refused to talk about the animal. To them it was a taboo topic.

Nguma-monene

NGAKOULA

Ngakoula is also called Chipekwe. It reaches a length of 50 feet and a weight of 4 tons or more. It preys on Hippopotamus, rhinoceros, and elephants. It is becoming very rare because the hippopotamus, rhinocerus, and elephants are becoming rare in its habitat.

Ngakoula reaches a length of 50 feet.

In 1932, John Johanson, a Swede, traveled with a guide, to the Kasai Valley in the Belgian Congo. They came across a rhinoceros and tried to get by it without being detected. Just then, a Ngakoula charged out of the underbrush and attacked the rhino. The guide ran and John fainted. When John recovered and woke up, the Ngakoula was eating the dead rhinoceros.

Also in 1932, a similar story appeared in the newspaper, the Rhodesian Herald. The Ngakoula was 40 to 50 feet in length.

Ngakoula eating a hippopotamus

John said the creature was reddish in colour and had blackish stripes. He maintained that it was a Tyrannosaurus Rex. Other people who have sighted the animal call it "Kasai Rex".

MBIELU-MBIELU-MBIELU

Cryptozoologist, Roy Mackai, went to the Likouala region of the Republic of the Congo. He collected stories from the natives about Mbielu-mbielu-mbielu. A few sightings were reported by the inhabitants of the villages of Bounila and Ebola. It is a herbivorous animal with planks growing out of its back. It has green algal growth covering its planks. Cryptozoologists have classified it as a Stegosauridae, most likely a Kentrosaurus.

MUHURU

(Artwork by Heinrich Harder 1858 - 1935)

This cryptid has been seen primarily in Kenya's jungles and is not known to be terribly aggressive. This animal is a stegosaurus and was believed to have been extinct for 150 million years. Muhuru is a herbivore.

26 FLYING DRAGONS

NAMBIAN FLYING SNAKE

The Nambian flying snake is found in the Karas region of Namibia, in Drakensburg, South Africa. It was seen in 1942 by Michael Esterhouise. He saw the massive snake hurl itself down a hill. He saw it again later, two more times. It was a yellow-brown with light spots.

The flying snake has been reported as being 9 to 25 feet long and is bioluminescent. The head has a crest and horns. It has a wing span of 30 feet. The Nambian flying snake does not glide but has a sustained flight which it begins by hurling itself down a hill. It makes a loud roaring sound.

The Nambian flying snake has a sustained flight

In 1942, the British cryptozoologist, Richard Muirhead, saw a flying snake swoop down from a cave near Kirris West. It left a trace of something on the ground and a burning smell.

In the 1960's a fisherman was killed by a flying dragon. He died 3 days after being attacked. His body was not just torn, it was also burned.

KONGAMATO

Frank Melland, in his book "Witchbound Africa", describes the Kongamato as living along certain rivers. He said it was very dangerous and often attacked small boats.

Biologist, Ivan T. Sanderson, had a close encounter with one in the 1930's.

In 1956, J. P. F. Brown saw the Kongamato at Fort Rosebery near Lake Bangweulu in Northern Rhodesia (now Zambia). At 6:30 p.m. he saw two Kongamato flying silently directly overhead. He estimated the wing span at 3 to 3 and a half feet. The beak to tail length was 4 and a half feet.

J. P. F. Brown saw two Kongamato flying silently (Artwork by Heinrich Harder 1858 - 1935)

In 1957, at a hospital in Fort Rosebery, a patient came in with a severe wound in his chest. A large bird like creature had attacked him in the Bangweulu swamps. The patient was asked to draw a picture of the creature which had attacked him. He drew a picture resembling a pterosaur.

The Kongamato is the native word for 'Breaker of Boats.' They are very aggressive and attack anyone who disturbs them.

The Kongamato have been reported in Kenya, Angola, Zimbabwe, Democratic Republic of the Congo, Namibia, and Tanzania.

Kongamata are very aggressive.

ROPEN

(photoshopped ropen by Karl G. Rose from enigmaticstatic.com)

The ropen was first sighted in 1935 by the famous biologist, Evelyn Cheesman, in Papua New Guinea. It has a wingspan of over 12 feet. It is thought to be a pterosaur. It has a tail length more than 25% of its wingspan. The ropen is bioluminescent and nocturnal. It lives on a diet of fish. It is thought that the bioluminescence attracts fish to the surface. Then, the ropen scoops the fish up from the surface by flying low over the water. This is similar to the technique used by pelicans.

Decades before the twentieth century, explorers described mysterious flying lights in the sky.

From 1994 to 2004, five expeditions went into Papua New Guinea to look for ropen. Only 3 sightings occurred from these expeditions.

In the mountainous area of Papua New Guinea around Tawa village was found a giant nocturnal flying creature. In November, 2006, the American investigator, Paul Nation found a colony of ropen.

Paul Nation found a colony of ropen

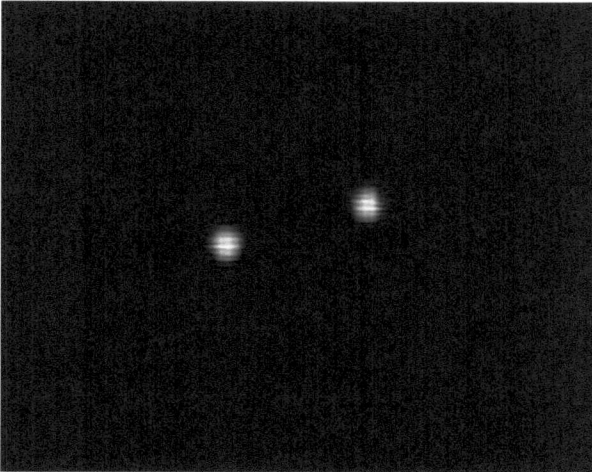

Paul Nation made video tapes of the ropen.

(Still photo from the Paul Nation video showing the bioluminescence of 2 ropen)

In 2006, an expedition made daylight observations of ropen.

A native from Pilo Island off the south-west coast of Papua New Guinea, Gibson Kuvurio, stated to investigators that the wawanar (ropen) is a dragon that 'owns the land and the sea'.

Ropen have been known to attack people. They also tear open graves and eat cadavers.

In the 1960s a fisherman was killed by a ropen. The man was not only cut but also burned.

Ropen is a dragon that 'owns the land and the sea'
(photoshopped ropen by Karl G. Rose from enigmaticstatic.com)

Jonathan Whitcomb, a pterosaur investigator, has analyzed much data from eye witnesses of ropen in both Papua New Guinea and the United States. Most witnesses describe a wing span of seven to nine feet. However, there were some of less than seven feet.

Critics state that these reports are a hoax. Whitcomb has found no evidence of a hoax. Critics of living pterosaur investigations have found no evidence of a hoax either.

UNITED STATES

Colorado, Utah, and New Mexico have stories of pterodactyl like creatures which go way back in time. The native people called them thunder birds.

Tombstone, Arizona is most famous for the gunfight at the OK corral. On April 26, 1880, the newspaper, the Tombstone Epitaph ran a story about two ranchers who found a huge flying creature between Whetstone and the Huachuca mountains. The creature was described as looking somewhat like an alligator with a long tail and bat like wings.

The creature seemed exhausted as the two men rode towards it. The creature (a pterodactyl) took off in short sporadic flights as the two ranchers kept pursuing it. Occasionally the men came close enough to fire on it with their rifles. The creature was wounded and kept flying away with short sporadic flights. Finally the pterodactyl turned on them. At that point the men were able to shoot it dead.

The ranchers reported that they had measured the creature. They said that the body was 92 feet in length. The wings from wing tip to wing tip measured 160 feet, and the head was 8 feet in length.

The story received much criticism because of the reported size of the beast. Nobody knows what happened to the carcass. The ranchers reported that they cut off a wing and sent it away for identification. But there is no record found of this claim. It was the habit of newspapers at that time to greatly exaggerate stories. Some people think that the story was a ploy to attract tourists to Tombstone.

The story continued to be debated. In 1966, a writer named Jack Pearl claimed that the story was true. He said that in 1886 the Tombstone Epitaph printed another story stating that a group of prospectors carried the dead monster into town and nailed it to a barn wall for a photograph. In the picture there are also six men standing with arms outstretched. The creature is estimated to be 36 feet from wing tip to wing tip.

Two of many pterodactyl photos taken in the area

The American civil war was fought from 1861 to 1865. A small group of Union soldiers sighted a pterodactyl. They shot and killed it. Then, they had their picture taken with the carcass.

Verified genuine image of a modern pterosaur — Declaration by Clifford Paiva (missile defense physicist) and Jonathan David Whitcomb (cryptozoology author)

From 1881 to 1886, there were many sightings of enormous flying creatures from the Elizabeth Lake area in California. The creature was often seen diving into the water and emerging with a fish in its mouth.

In 2011 a man from Phoenix, Arizona reported that he had seen a large bird like creature with no feathers, leathery wings and a huge thing at the back of its head. It landed in a river and splashed around.

In 2012, another man claimed he saw a baby Pterodactyl under a bridge in Tucson, Arizona. It had a wing span of about

8 feet. It was covered in white fur and had a top knot which was molting. As witnesses approached, the creature took an attack stance, spread its wings and hissed loudly.

In 1999, a lady in north Atlanta Georgia saw a flying pterodactyl. Her neighbours had, on other occasions in 1999, also seen the creature. The lady's brother at another time also saw the flying pterodactyl. Many people have seen the flying pterodactyl but refused to report it.

At 11:45 a.m. on November 14, 2012, Professor Steven Watters saw a featherless long-tailed flying creature in Crestview, Florida.

Biology professor, Peter Beach, has been searching for bioluminescent pterosaurs reported flying regularly over a river in Washington state.

In June, 2017, a boy and his mother were in their backyard in Draper, Utah when they saw a dragon fly overhead.

Crypto zoologists state that dragon sightings are not rare, but people refuse to report them because of fear of ridicule.

CANADA

In July, 2015, a family in their backyard in Edmonton, Alberta saw a pterodactyl. The dragon was just flying slowly over the strip mall directly behind their house. It had very short feet. The tail was long and skinny with a spade shape at its end.

In the fall of 2016, near the town of Lindsay, Ontario, a man saw a flying creature, At first he thought it was a blue heron. It launched from a high tree top from the south-east corner where the Scugog River and Highway 7 intersect. The creature turned out to be a pterodactyl.

In a park in Brampton, Ontario a young mother and her children saw large featherless "birds" perch themselves in a tree near her. She became afraid of the creatures and left the park in a hurry.

One November morning near Brampton, Kevin Meisner and his mother saw a strange bird like creature flying about 20 feet from their car. It was gray, featherless, and had a wing span of about 4 feet. It also had a long skinny pointed tail ending in a diamond shaped knot at the tip.

There have been many ropen sightings in British Columbia.

27 RIVER DRAGONS

In the 1930s a family was traveling west. They stopped and made a camp. A small, bipedal, dinosaur came into camp looking for food. The family fed it. The creature came back the next night and the next night. After several nights, the father captured it and put it in a bird cage. They took the creature with them. When the creature became too big for the bird cage, they transferred it to a larger cage. When that cage became too small, they again transferred it to a larger cage. Finally, the bipedal dinosaur became too big to keep. The family drove it back to the old camp site and released it. It ran off on its two legs very fast with its head way out in front and its tail straight back.

In Colorado there have been many reports of theropod dinosaurs about 3.5 feet tall and 7 feet long. They have very powerful hind legs. Their fore legs are mere appendages. They lurk in wet environments near water. They are called Mini T Rexs, River Dinos, or sometimes River Lizards.

A man in Pueblo, Colorado had been dirt bike riding with a friend. They saw a strange creature moving through a clearing ahead of them. He described it as a reptilian creature about 4 feet long. The colour was greenish with black markings on its back and orange colouring on its under belly. It walked fast on its hind legs without dragging its tail. The front legs were significantly shorter than its hind legs and had 3 or 4 claws. The creature let out a high-pitched shriek when it saw the men. The men claimed that another friend had also come upon the beast and had taken pictures. The pictures were sent to cryptozoologist Chad Arnebt for identification. Unfortunately, the pictures were grainy and of poor quality. Other pictures were also sent to Chad Arment. One shows a man with a rifle and a small dead River Dino.

Man with rifle and a small, dead River Dino

In Colorado in 2001, Shannon Ystesund was driving her car with her daughter. They saw a deer dart across the road in front of them. Shannon put on the brakes and it was apparent that the creature was not a deer.

The creature was about 3 feet tall, with a long slender neck, skinny legs, and small arms. It ran gracefully on its two legs. It seemed bird-like, but it was no bird. It had no feathers. Ystesund and her daughter were convinced they had seen a miniature dinosaur. Shannon told her story to cryptozoologist, Nick Sucik.

Myrtle Snow, a resident of Pagosa Springs, Colorado claims that she has seen small dinosaurs on many occasions during her lifetime. She first saw them when she was a little girl in the 1930s. She saw 5 baby bipedal dinosaurs.

Myrtle saw 5 baby bipedal dinosaurs

A farmer in the area had sheep killed by a mysterious animal. The killings stopped after he shot a bipedal dinosaur that was 7 feet long. The carcass was put on ice and shipped to Denver Museum. But the carcass never arrived at the museum.

Snow, in later years, spotted another one running along the road while she was driving, and says she saw yet another one in a cave. She related several of these experiences in a letter to the Rocky Mountain Empire Magazine in 1982.

In 1996, a woman in Mesa Verde, California reported looking out her front door and seeing a large lizard that was three and a half feet tall and three and a half feet long and was standing on two legs.   It moved very rapidly towards a nearby pond.

It moved very rapidly towards a nearby pond

A couple from Cortez, Colorado were visiting in Arizona. They came across a toy dinosaur. When it moved, they realized that it was not a toy.

28 STATISTICS OF DRAGONS

Cryptozoologist, Jonathan Whitcomb, has been collecting sightings of dragons (pterodactyls, ropens, and other dinosaurs). He states that he has at least 1400 reports from credible witnesses in the U.S.A. Many witnesses talked about their sightings to friends and neighbours. Most of these witnesses stated that 4 or 5 of these friends or neighbours said to the witnesses that they too had seen a dragon. Thus Jonathan estimated that the number 1400 may be expanded to 5 or 10 times. Therefore, his estimate from this is 14,000 witnesses. This is a very small proportion of the population in the United States which has a population of over 326 million people.

There are reports of dragon (dinosaur) sightings from every continent except for Antarctica. It is amazing how many sightings there are of creatures that became extinct 65 million years ago. Our skies are full of dinosaurs. The birds evolved from the dinosaurs. Modern birds are said to have come into existence 65 to 60 million years ago. This is quite a feat and clashes with the extinction event of 65 million years ago. It is difficult to evolve from something which is extinct.

Dinosaurs (the modern dragons) are being sighted today, but they are hard to find. They require their own specialized habitats. The Nessies are found in deep cold lakes. Some dragons are found only in Cameroon or the Congo. Some are found only in Papua New Guinea.

Even when we know where their habitats are, they are not seen very often. Many people who have searched for dragons in their natural habitat have been disappointed. The dragons are elusive and do not want to be seen.

A few people have been lucky enough to catch sight of Nessie, Ogopogo, Champ, and Puff. However, when people happen to come across other dragons, they are amazed and sometimes frightened.

Science has identified about 2 million species of plants, animals and microbes on Earth, but scientists estimate there are still millions more left to discover. New species are constantly being discovered, described and cataloged. Every year brings new discoveries into the encyclopedia of life.

CARSTEN R. JORGENSEN

REFERENCES

Books:

Coleman, Loren. and Huyghe, Patrick. *The Field Guide To lake Monsters, Sea Serpents, And Other Denziens Of The Deep.* Penguin Group, 2003.

Marshall, Richard. *Mysteries of the Unexplained.* Edited by Carroll C Calkins, Reader's Digest Association Inc., 1982.

Bible NIV Daniel 14:23-42

Polo, Marco and Rustichello of Pisa. *The Travels of Marco Polo — Volume 2.* New York: Signet Classics, 1961.
Retreived from
http://www.gutenberg.org/ebooks/12410

Shuker, Karl. *Dragons: A Natural History.* Simon & Schuster, 1995.

Dickinson, Peter. *The Flight Of Dragons.* Pierrot Publishing Ltd, 1979.

Jorgensen, Carsten R. *The Saga Kings.* 2015.

Videos:

Last Chance To See (episode 4). Directed by John Paul Davidson, performance by Mark Carwardine and Stephen Fry, BBC. BBC Two, 2009. www.netflix.com/ca/title/70140511

Websites:

Redfern, Nick (2011, November 7) *Chasing The Dragon*
Retreived from
http://mysteriousuniverse.org/2011/11/chasing-the-dragon/

Klien, Darius Matthias (2008, August 26) *Athanasius Kircher's Natural History Of Dragons*. Retreived from http://christianlatin.blogspot.ca/2008/08/athanasius-kirchers-natural-history-of.html

Simon, Matt (2014, May 16) *Absurd Creature Of The Week: This Beetle Fires Boiling Chemicals Out Of Its Bum*. Retreived from https://www.wired.com/2014/05/absurd-creature-of-the-week-bombardier-beetle/

Mowbray, Sean (2017, October 7) *The Story Behind Switzerland's Dragon-Slaying Saint*. Retreived from https://theculturetrip.com/europe/switzerland/articles/the-story-behind-switzerlands-dragon-slaying-saint/

Horsham Photography (2014, August 25) *The Dragon In St Leonard's Forest* . Retreived from https://horshamphotography.wordpress.com/2014/08/25/the-dragon-in-st-leonards-forest/

Wu Mingren (2016, April 30) *Exploring The famous Legend Of Saint George And The Dragon*. Retreived from http://www.ancient-origins.net/history-famous-people/exploring-famous-legend-st-george-and-dragon-005794

Marit Synnøve Vea / Nordvegen Historiesenter. *Norway's Oldest Royal Seat Avaldsnes*. Retreived from http://avaldsnes.info/en/informasjon/olav-tryggvason/

Valdar (2016, July 14) *Slithering Through the Stories of Ancient Snake Deities: Serpent Gods of Ancient Mythology*. Retreived from http://www.ancient-origins.net/myths-legends/ancient-snake-deities-gods-ancient-mythology-006282

Wikipedia. *The dragon (Beowulf)*. Retreived from https://en.wikipedia.org/wiki/The_dragon_(Beowulf)

Wikipedia. *Heinrich von Winkelried.* Retreived from
https://en.wikipedia.org/wiki/Heinrich_von_Winkelried

Has Colonel Fawcett's Giant Snake been found? Retreived from
http://www.fawcettadventure.com/colonel-fawcett's-giant-
snake.html

Micah Hanks.(2017, April 30) *The Mother of the Water: In Search of
Percy Fawcett's 'Monster' Anaconda.* Retreived from
http://mysteriousuniverse.org/2017/04/the-mother-of-the-
water-in-search-of-percy-fawcetts-monster-anaconda/

Nick Redfern (2016, October 3) *Close Encounters With Giant
Snakes.* Retreived from
http://mysteriousuniverse.org/2016/10/close-encounters-with-
giant-snakes/

Denver Michaels (2017, November) *Colossal Snakes Of The
Amazon.* Retreived from
http://www.denvermichaels.net/wp-
content/uploads/2017/11/sample.pdf

Kyle Butt (2008) *Marco Polo's Dragons* Retreived from
https://www.apologeticspress.org/APContent.aspx?
category=9&article=2562

Chinese Dragons. Retreived from
http://www.crystalinks.com/chinadragons.html

Quetzalcoatl . Retreived from
http://www.crystalinks.com/quetzalcoatl.html

Tom Mullen (2015, February 26) *Sir Richard Owen: The Man Who
Invented The Dinosaur.* Retreived from
http://www.bbc.com/news/uk-england-lancashire-31623397

About The Chicxulub Crater. Retreived from
http://www.chicxulubcrater.org/

The Associated Press (2018, May 23) *Legend Of Loch Ness Monster To be Tested With DNA.*
Retreived from
http://torontosun.com/news/world/legend-of-loch-ness-monster-will-be-tested-with-dna-samples/wcm/4f34b878-58ad-42e5-a8de-993e17e57943

Wikipedia. *List Of Reported Lake Monsters.* Retreived from
https://en.wikipedia.org/wiki/List_of_reported_lake_monsters

Darrin Naish (2017, March 16) *The Soay Island Sea Monster of 1959.* Retreived from
https://blogs.scientificamerican.com/tetrapod-zoology/the-soay-island-sea-monster-of-1959/

Mokele-Mbembe. Retreived from
www.angelfire.com/freak2/demonoverlord_7290/mokele.htm

Bellows, Jason. (2005, December 10) *The Tracks Of The Mokele-Mbembe.* Retreived from www.damninteresting.com/retired/the-tracks-of-the-mokl-mbmb/

André. (2015, January 22) *Mokele-Mbembe.* Retreived from
http://verdadedosdinossauros.blogspot.ca/2015/01/mokele-mbembe.html

(2018, March 11) *Mokele-Mbembe - Freshwater Monster – ALPF Medical Research.* Retreived from
www.alpfmedical.info/freshwater-monster/
mokelembembe.html

Woetzel, Dave. (1999 – 2018) *Mokele-mbembe of the Congo.* Retreived from www.genesispark.com/exhibits/evidence/cryptozoological/apa tosaurs/mokele-mbembe

Woetzel, Dave. (1999 – 2018) *Emela-ntouka of the Congo.* Retreived from www.genesispark.com/exhibits/evidence/cryptozoological/cer atopsian/emela-ntouka/

Kirk, Johm (2006, April 9) *The Ngoubou.* Retreived from http://cryptomundo.com/cryptotourism/ngoubou/

Drinnon, Dale A. (2011, April 19) *Congo Dragons And The Colossal Confusions Over The Colossal Beasts.* Retreived from http://cryptidchronicles.tumblr.com/post/19547009190/cong o-dragons-and-the-colossal-confusions-over-the-colos

Whitcomb, Jonathan David (2007–2017) *Results of Investigations Concerning Pterosaur Sightings In Papua New Guinea : Computer Image Processing of the Paul Nation Video (Including Characterization of Pterosaur Optics, Flight Dynamics, and Bioluminescence).* Retreived from http://www.ropens.com/report/pg-01/

O'Brien, Christopher (2017, January 19) *Modern Dinos?* Retreived from https://www.ourstrangeplanet.com/modern-dinos/

Parker, Chris (2017, January 19) *Man And Dinosaur Co-existence.* Retreived from http://s8int.com/articles/13/19/Colorado-River-Dinosaur-Mini-T-rex.htm

ABOUT THE AUTHOR

Carsten Jorgensen dedicated thirty years in studying and managing fisheries for the Ontario Ministry of Natural Resources.

Upon graduation from Queen's University in Kingston, Ontario in 1966, he accepted a biologist position on Lake Temagami with the Ontario Department of Lands and Forests.

In 1968 he also started work on Lake Nipissing. In 1970, Mr. Jorgensen was working full time as the Lake Nipissing Fisheries Assessment Unit Biologist.

In 1970 he married Brenda Black, daughter of Ontario Conservation Officer, Gordon Black.

In 1996 he retired and now enjoys spending his time playing chess, playing darts, doing Tai Chi, and writing books.

OTHER TITLES BY CARSTEN R. JORGENSEN

If you enjoyed this book by Carsten R. Jorgensen, you may also enjoy these other books that he has written:

The Saga Kings
ISBN-13: 978-09949338-0-5

Trying To Work For The M.N.R.
ISBN-13: 978-0-9949338-1-2

My World War Two Adventures In Denmark
ISBN-13: 978-0-9949338-2-9

One School, Two School, Old School, New School
ISBN-13: 978-0-9949338-3-6

Spiritual Encounters And Other Strange Stories From The Little Red School-house
ISBN-13: 978-0-9938776-3-6

Fishes Of Lake Nipissing
ISBN-13: 978-0-9949338-4-3

Or check out his author profile on Good Reads for any new and upcoming books he may be working on:

www.goodreads.com/author/show/14680643.Carsten_R_Jorgensen